A UNIQUE COLLECTION OF POEMS
WITH DESIGNS TO COLOR

POEMS BY: JAMES B. KOCKLER

ILLUSTRATIONS BY: JILL PETTIGREW

RESOURCE *Publications* · Eugene, Oregon

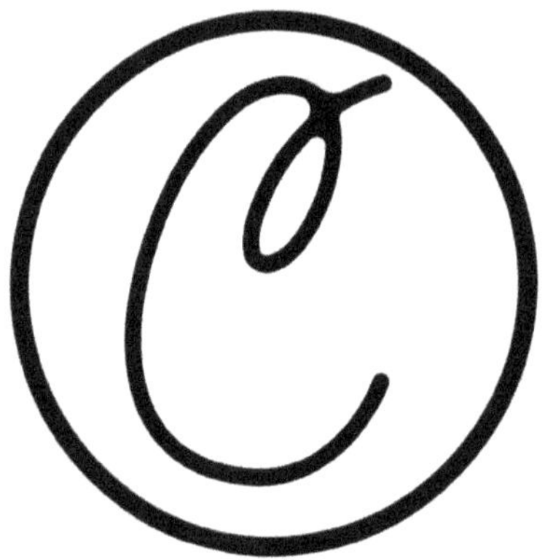

LOOK UP

A Unique Collection of Poems with Designs to Color

Resource Publications
An Imprint of Wipf and Stock Publishers
199 W. 8th Ave., Suite 3
Eugene, OR 97401

www.wipfandstock.com

paperback isbn: 979-8-3852-7964-7
hardcover isbn: 979-8-3852-7965-4
ebook isbn: 979-8-3852-7966-1

LOOK UP

A UNIQUE COLLECTION OF POEMS WITH DESIGNS TO COLOR

STEP INTO A WORLD OF COLOR, POETRY, AND FAITH!
THIS FATHER/DAUGHTER COLLABORATION BRINGS TOGETHER
JAMES' HEARTFELT WORDS AND JILL'S ORIGINAL HAND-DRAWN ART.
EACH ILLUSTRATION GROWS FROM THE LETTERS OF ITS POEM'S TITLE,
READY FOR YOU TO COLOR WITH CRAYONS, COLORED PENCILS, OR MARKERS.
RELAX, CREATE, AND REFLECT ON THE BEAUTY OF LIFE, GOD'S GLORY,
AND THE GOSPEL OF JESUS CHRIST ONE POEM AT A TIME!

TIP: IF YOU'RE COLORING WITH MARKERS, PLACE A PIECE OF CARDBOARD OR HEAVY CARDSTOCK UNDERNEATH YOUR PAGE SO THE INK DOESN'T BLEED THROUGH TO THE NEXT SHEET !

ENJOY!

JIM & JILL

* This book is a work of poetry, and while drawing inspiration from Biblical themes, it is not the inspired Word of God. It is meant for edification and encouragement, not as a replacement for Scripture. Readers are encouraged to read the Scripture for themselves and apply it to their lives.

This book is dedicated, first and foremost,
to Jesus, the Christ, my Lord and Savior.

Then, to my family: Shirley, Jim, Jeff & Jill,
who have been tremendously helpful
and supportive in this endeavor;
especially Jill,
who has done the bulk
of the work to accomplish this—
her influence and inspiration
has made this all possible.

"Now when these things begin to happen,
look up and lift up your heads,
because your redemption draws near."
~ Jesus Christ

(Luke 21:28 NKJV)

POEM TITLES

LOOK UP
When you're
out in the world,
what do you see?
Are you watching
your phone,
or do you see
the trees?
Look up!
and see a bird
as it flies by,
or watch a jet
as it makes
a contrail
across the sky,
or just watch
the clouds
as they roll by.
At night
you can
look up
and see the stars.
They tell me
there are
even times
you can see Mars.
Look up!
and see the world
out there,
there's some
beautiful things;
or... do you
just not care?
The wind,
you can't see—
but you can
feel the breeze.
Look up!
and watch
as it ruffles
the leaves.
Look up!
at the people
as you walk along,
you may notice
a smile,
and that
can't be wrong.
Look up!
to your elders,
who are worthy
of respect;
treat everyone fairly,
and you'll
have no regrets.
As the end
is getting nearer,
it's becoming
increasingly clearer.
Jesus said,
"Have no fear-
Look up!
and lift your head,
because your
redemption
draws near."
So with
your final
Look up!
when Jesus returns,
you'll be
satisfied forever
for what you've
just learned.

ME & YOU

When I was just a little boy,
I heard this old-time story
that brought great joy.
It's an old story
I know is true,
'cause it's all about me and you.

You see, a baby was born in an animal pen,
it wasn't real sanitary but that's how it was back then.
As He grew up, He always knew,
that someday, He'd go to the cross
for me and you.
He grew up strong and pure in God's sight,
He never sinned in day or night.
At about 30 his ministry began,
it wouldn't last long, but that was the plan.

He did what He had to,
remember, it was for me and you.

He had twelve friends and one was fake,
this happened as a lesson for our sake.
They beat Him so bad, He almost died,
people watched and the women cried.
He took these stripes to provide our healing,
that's a Biblical truth, not just a feeling.
Although it was hard,
He did what He had to do.

And He did it all,
for me and you.

Then came the worst part, His death on the cross,
He did it all so we wouldn't be lost,
He did this, despite the cost.
He there, paid the price for all of our sins,
what's amazing about this,
is that He would do it again.
He did it for us,
it's what He had to do,

Remember, He did it all,
for me and you.

When we get to heaven and see Him face to face,
we will know we're in the perfect place.
We'll look around and see people we knew,
then we'll know,
it wasn't only
for me and you.

SALVATION
What are you going to do
when it's your time to die?
Some people are happy and others will cry.
What's going to happen to my body and soul?
Have I done enough, have I reached my goal?
I've gone to church often, especially when it was sunny,
I've prayed a lot, I even gave money.
What else was I supposed to do?
I'm as good as anyone else, even better than a few.
If God is fair, I think He'll say I'm okay—
I hope for my sake, it all works out that way.
If these are your thoughts, you've got it all wrong,
if you've placed your faith in Jesus, then you belong.
He's the only way.
He's the truth and the life.
So keep searching for Him, until you see the light.
Salvation's a gift, you have to receive
Jesus said to us,
"Simply Believe".

THE PLAN

Father,
what do you want me to do?
Whatever it is, I'll do it for you.
Well, in the beginning Son, we created a plan,
you knew it was necessary for you to become a man.
Because Adam and Eve turned out not so nice,
it's going to mean you'll have to pay the price.
And we know it'll be a hard thing to do,
but once it's done, they can put their faith in you.
We'll send preachers and laymen to spread the word,
so no one can say, "I never heard."
We'll give them plenty of chances to determine their fate,
you can return here with me, and then we'll wait.
We'll send down the Spirit to those who believe,
and we'll encourage all of them to receive.
There will always be some who won't understand,
but it's worth it to try, because that's our plan.
If you're one of those who don't make the choice—
to worship Jesus while you have a voice,
I ask you respectfully to accept Him now,
because to get to heaven,
that's exactly how.

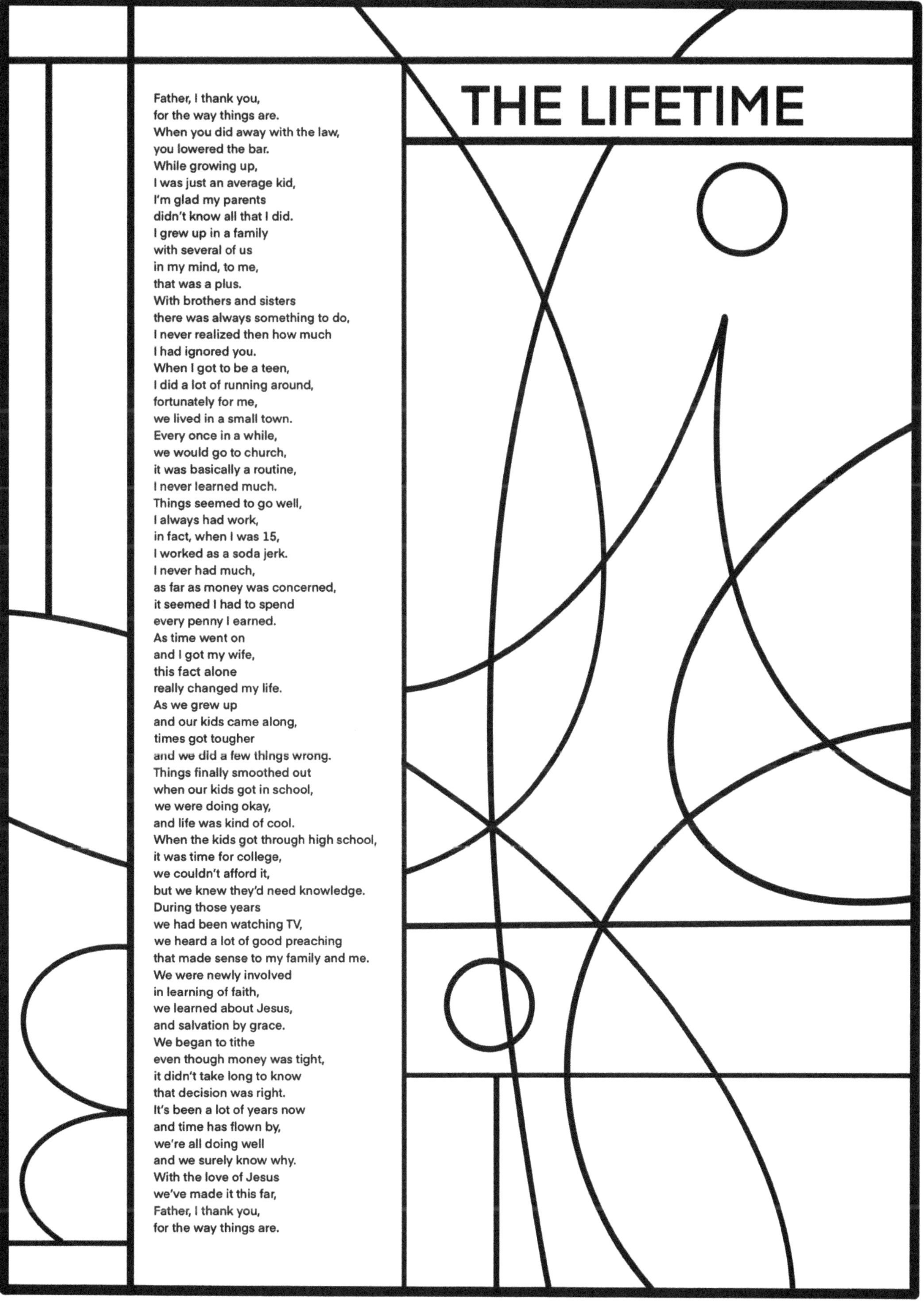

THE LIFETIME

Father, I thank you,
for the way things are.
When you did away with the law,
you lowered the bar.
While growing up,
I was just an average kid,
I'm glad my parents
didn't know all that I did.
I grew up in a family
with several of us
in my mind, to me,
that was a plus.
With brothers and sisters
there was always something to do,
I never realized then how much
I had ignored you.
When I got to be a teen,
I did a lot of running around,
fortunately for me,
we lived in a small town.
Every once in a while,
we would go to church,
it was basically a routine,
I never learned much.
Things seemed to go well,
I always had work,
in fact, when I was 15,
I worked as a soda jerk.
I never had much,
as far as money was concerned,
it seemed I had to spend
every penny I earned.
As time went on
and I got my wife,
this fact alone
really changed my life.
As we grew up
and our kids came along,
times got tougher
and we did a few things wrong.
Things finally smoothed out
when our kids got in school,
we were doing okay,
and life was kind of cool.
When the kids got through high school,
it was time for college,
we couldn't afford it,
but we knew they'd need knowledge.
During those years
we had been watching TV,
we heard a lot of good preaching
that made sense to my family and me.
We were newly involved
in learning of faith,
we learned about Jesus,
and salvation by grace.
We began to tithe
even though money was tight,
it didn't take long to know
that decision was right.
It's been a lot of years now
and time has flown by,
we're all doing well
and we surely know why.
With the love of Jesus
we've made it this far,
Father, I thank you,
for the way things are.

FAITH
Faith is not a feeling,
it's what you believe.
It's a resource you can use,
whenever you choose.
It can get you where
you want to go,
walking on paths
you don't even know.
It can provide a way,
when there seems
to be none,
it can bring special results
to anyone.
When you study the Word,
your faith will grow,
but in order to reap,
you first have to sow.
You have to eliminate doubt,
and it will all work out.
A mustard seed amount
is all it takes,
and for you to use it,
it only takes faith.

A day with the Lord
is like a thousand years.

A concept to us,
that's hard to understand.

We seem to count days
in 24 hours,
we limit the Lord
and all of His powers.
He made heaven and earth
and all of the stars,
He made all the planets
including Mars.
But His greatest creation
was mortal man,
that was good in His sight,
His primary plan.
He created us for
His own pleasure,
we were intended to be
His peculiar treasure.
It started out fine
as time was going along,
until Adam and Eve
did what was wrong.
Then Cain slew Abel
one day in his wrath,
that continued mankind
down the wrong path.
It got so bad
after that time,
that God brought a flood
to end all the crime.
As time went on
the Lord continued His plan,
He sent His own Son
to try to save man.
It's sad today
that many still don't believe,
but it's not too late,
if they'll only receive.
Nobody knows
how many days are left,
today is the day of salvation,
so accept the gift.
A DAY WITH THE LORD

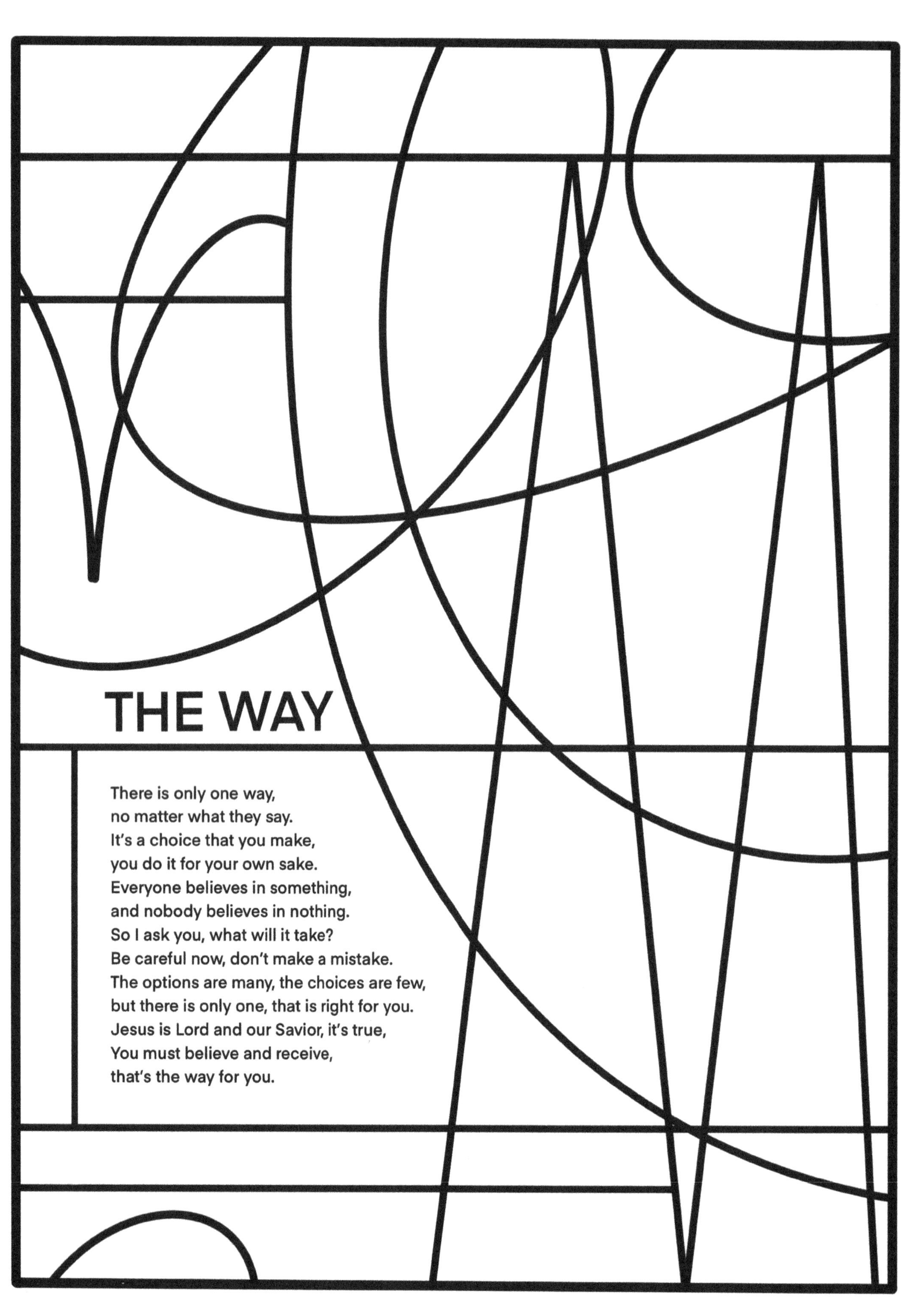

THE WAY

There is only one way,
no matter what they say.
It's a choice that you make,
you do it for your own sake.
Everyone believes in something,
and nobody believes in nothing.
So I ask you, what will it take?
Be careful now, don't make a mistake.
The options are many, the choices are few,
but there is only one, that is right for you.
Jesus is Lord and our Savior, it's true,
You must believe and receive,
that's the way for you.

Time is fleeting, it goes by fast.
When it comes to living, we hope it will last.
It seems to go slowly when you're very young,
but as you age you ask, where has it gone?
When you're waiting for events, it seems to go slow,
you'll soon be asking, where did it go?
Everyone is so busy doing their thing,
sometimes it's work, sometimes a fling.
We all have standards, we all have goals,
the most important of these, is saving our souls.
Some people feel they must work to achieve,
but Jesus said, "We only need to believe."
He did all the work when He went to the cross,
He paid for all our sins, so we wouldn't be lost.
Time is passing,
so what are you going to do?
He did it for all,
and that includes you.
TIME

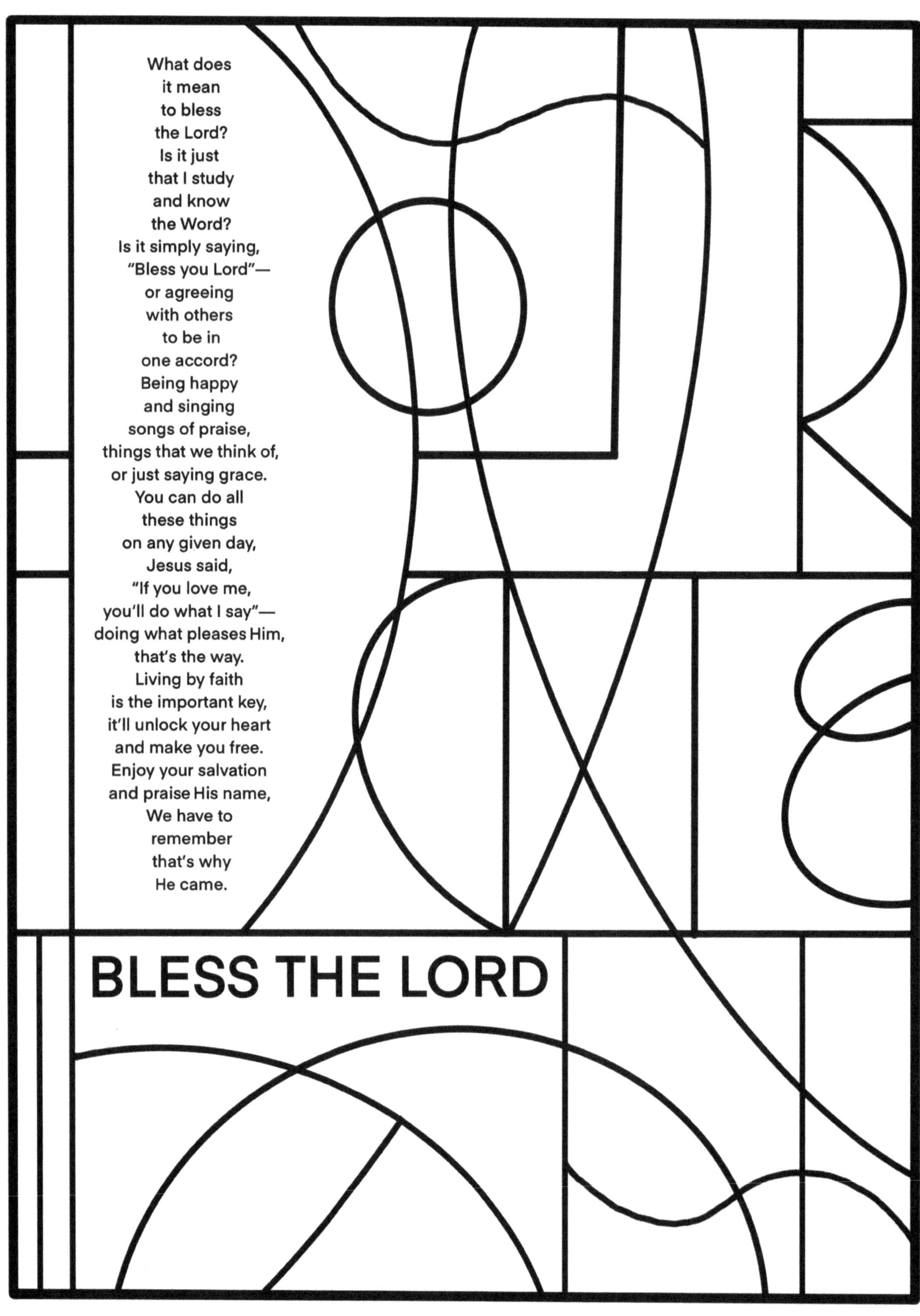
What does
it mean
to bless
the Lord?
Is it just
that I study
and know
the Word?
Is it simply saying,
"Bless you Lord"—
or agreeing
with others
to be in
one accord?
Being happy
and singing
songs of praise,
things that we think of,
or just saying grace.
You can do all
these things
on any given day,
Jesus said,
"If you love me,
you'll do what I say"—
doing what pleases Him,
that's the way.
Living by faith
is the important key,
it'll unlock your heart
and make you free.
Enjoy your salvation
and praise His name,
We have to
remember
that's why
He came.
BLESS THE LORD

PEACE
Peace
can be a feeling
or a state of mind.
It can stop your anger and make you kind.
It can calm your nerves when you feel upset.
It can minimize your troubles and let you forget.
It can bring you comfort when you need it the most,
it's a decision you make, it's really a choice.
Jesus said, "My peace I give to you",
so tap into that - it's all you have to do,
resist the devil and he'll flee from you.
You may face temptation, but don't give in.
I read the back of the book,
and in the end—
we win!

TEMPTATION

Have you
ever been told
to do what is right?
Either during the day,
or especially at night.
For that to apply,
suggests there's a choice,
if it's a parent who told you,
will you heed their voice?
When temptation comes
to draw you in,
will you stick to
your principles,
or commit to sin?
The choice will be yours,
so what will you do,
with no one else
to blame,
it's all up to you.
It's right or wrong,
with no in between,
you either do what's right,
or become unclean.
After all
is said and done,
was it really important,
or just for fun?
Mistakes can happen,
it's sad but true,
but if you'll just
follow Jesus,
He'll take care of you.

TROUBLES

You get up in the morning, and you feel okay.
You get dressed, and you're ready to have a good day.
You go to work and work hard for your pay.
You've known for years it's got to be this way.
You've been with this company and want to stay.
You think about a pension and getting old and grey.

You're on your lunch break and hear a lot of sound,
it's very unusual, you wonder what's going down.
A few minutes later, the boss comes around.
He says, "The company's been sold and moving out of town,
use the rest of the day to clean out your gear,
because after tomorrow, you won't be allowed in here."

What do you do when the bottom drops out?
You can yell and scream, or sit down and pout.
But you've trusted in the Lord, that it will all work out.
You know He's been with you, through all these years,
He'll not forsake you, so have no fear.
Let not your heart be troubled, don't shed a tear.

Listen to me people,
to what I say,
I'm going to tell you
how to have a great day—
whether staying at home
or going away.
You need to clear your mind
of any negative thoughts,
then thank the Lord
for all the things you've got.
They may be few,
or they may be a lot.
In any event,
you're still alive,
He's given you air
to breathe,
so you can survive.
You've got eyes to see
and ears to hear,
with your spiritual heart,
you know He's near.
As you go through the day
on your normal walk,
if you listen closely,
you can hear Him talk.
He'll give you insight
and show you the way,
rest assured,
He'll not lead you astray.

Follow Jesus -
and have a great day!

A GREAT DAY

PROVISION

He created the stars,
the trees and the grass,
He made them well,
so they'd be sure to last.

He made the springs to trickle,
the rivers to go fast,
He created the air
out of oxygen and gas —
we're using them now,
as they did in the past.

Ships use the stars
to show the way,
trees we burn,
on a cold winter's day.
The grass we cut,
to feed cattle with hay.

Water we drink,
and irrigate our lands.
The air we breathe,
can slip right through our hands.

There's nothing we need,
that He did not provide,

Praise God!
I'm so glad
I'm along for the ride!

A GOLDEN CHAIN

Christianity is like
a golden chain.
It always has been,
and will always remain.

It all starts with grace
that's given by God.

Then comes conviction,
by hearing the Word.

Next comes commitment,
by faith in what you've heard.

That creates salvation,
the fourth link in the chain.

Fifth comes justification,
you receive with no strain.

Then comes sanctification,
there's no work to obtain.

Eventually glorification,
will be our refrain.

At this final process,
you'll know you've attained,
your place with Jesus,
where you'll always remain.

Listen very carefully,
I've got good news for you,
if you think you can
work your way to heaven,
you haven't a clue.

Salvation is the free gift,
given by God.
If you don't believe that,
just read His Word.

He said, "You must be
born from above",
He made it easy for us,
because of His love.

You don't have to
climb up any hills,
take any medication
or special pills.

You only have to
really believe,
in Jesus the Christ,
then you will receive.
He did all the work
when He went to the cross,
you put your faith in Him,
and let God be the boss.

It's not about money
or labor—
there is no cost.

Trust me in this,
and you won't be lost.

GOOD NEWS

THE TREE

A tree
can stand tall
through thick and thin,
some can withstand
hurricane winds.

They can live through the cold
and survive the winter,
they can deliver a lot of pain,
with only a sliver.

As cold as it gets,
their sap does not freeze,
when springtime comes,
they sprout their leaves.
They thrive through the summer,
and wait for fall,
some become lumber,
fortunately not all.

The tree provides a lesson
we can all learn,
stand tall and straight
and never turn.

For,
if you don't hold
your ground—

you might get burned.

HEAVEN

Many people believe
that heaven's not real,
I'll tell you right now,
that's not how I feel.
I believe in Jesus
and all the things He taught,
He said, "He's the Only Way",
that's all we got.

He said, "There's only two roads,
one narrow, and one wide" —
It's either all true,
or else Jesus lied.

He fulfilled all
that was prophesied,
I'll take His word for it —
I'm on His side.

They say there are many ways;
but that's a false teaching —
here in the last days.

He's been here before,
and I know He'll come back,
His second coming will be
with a mighty attack.
He'll eliminate His enemies
and rule and reign,
for all the people on earth
there'll be terrible pain.
For a thousand years,
He'll be fully in charge,
there'll be no opposition,
neither small nor large.

At the very end,
Satan will have one last fling,
one more chance,
to do his thing.
Then, he'll be cast
into the lake of fire,
to end his action forever,
which was not his desire.

Jesus will enter eternity
to rule and reign,
where we'll worship and praise Him,
again and again.

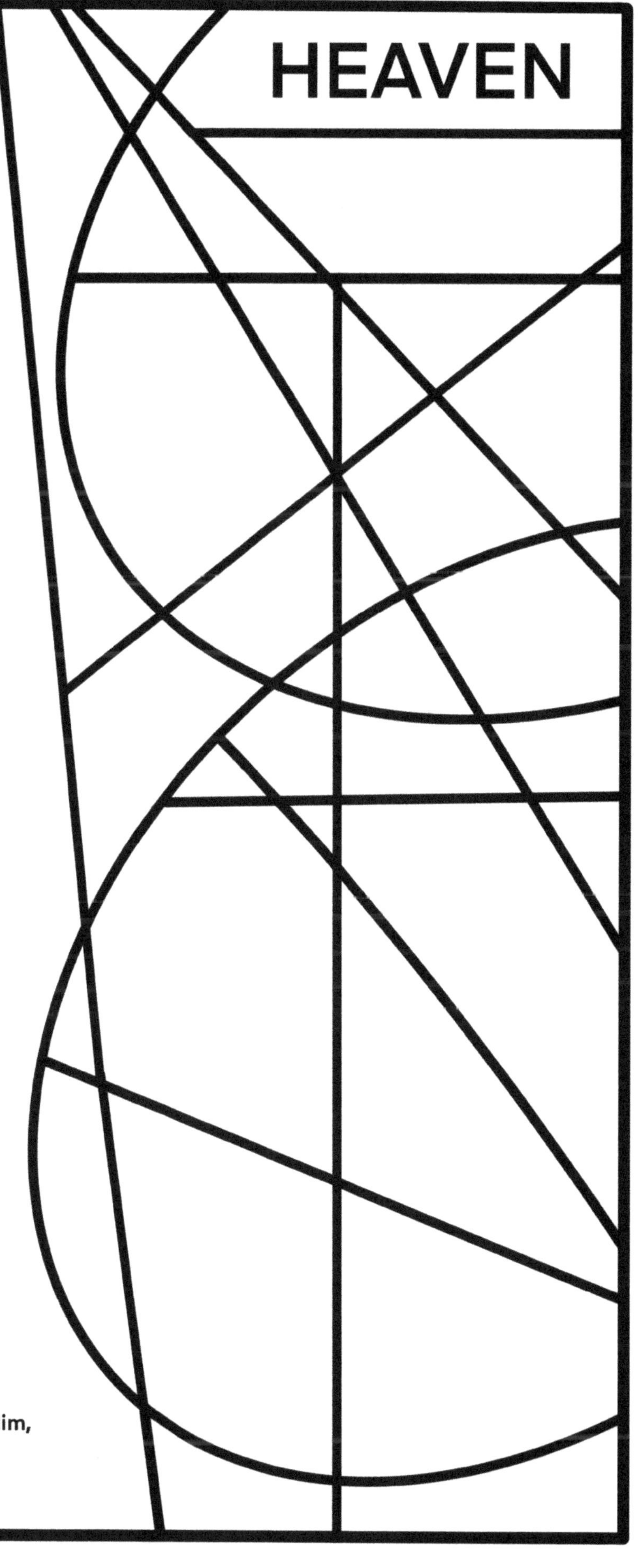

THE WEATHER

There will always be weather,
whether you like it or not.

It can be cold and snowing
or blistering hot.
The rain can come down
in great big drops,
or come down gently
to water our crops.
It can cause streams and rivers
to overflow,
but if we didn't have water
nothing would grow.
It mostly rains
in the spring and fall,
that's perfect for farm crops
to grow big and tall.
In the drier seasons
they have to irrigate,
but to get the desired results,
it's worth the wait.
In the winter
rain turns to snow or sleet,
if you like winter sports
it can be really neat.
But snow can reek havoc
on many of our roads,
causing accidents
and even trucks
to lose their loads.
Kids enjoy sledding
and going downhill,
but they have to dress warm
to avoid the chill.
Working in the cold
makes everything harder,
using hammers and nails
and even a battery charger.
Whatever it is,
we have to cope,
but one thing for sure,
we always have hope.

There will always be weather,
whether you like it or not.

DIRECTION

Direction is generally a way to go,
most times it's determined by what you know.
Sometimes depending on what's your goal,
if you want to play
in a starring role.

Work can be an important part,
but sometimes you just have to
follow your heart.
Oftentimes, you can make a choice,
sometimes you can even have a voice—
in a decision about
what you should do,
especially when it involves
more than just you.
Included in this is right and wrong,
you must consider
where you belong.

It's wise to seek experienced advice—
if it's someone you know and respect,
that would be especially nice.

When it comes to salvation,
by Jesus,
by grace,
You can be sure of your direction
by using your faith.

Promises are made for keeping, when they come from the heart—
whenever you make a promise, you must keep your part.
When you give your word and make a vow, you must fulfill it
no matter how. Your word is your bond, it must be true,
it depends on your character, it's the real you.
The Lord promised Abram many things,
He'd never forsake him, no matter
what this life brings.
He'd give him land
and his own nation,
He'll never break His promise,
it's His reputation. You can read the prophets
and understand what they said, you can validate it's truth,
if you know what you've read. It'll stay that way forever, it will never end.
He'll keep His word to Abraham, He called him His friend.

PROMISES

THE LAMB'S BOOK OF LIFE

Is your name written
in the Lamb's Book of Life?
You can make sure it's there
with no trouble or strife.
It's very simple,
it's easy to do,
Jesus went to the cross
to provide it for you.
Religion won't do it,
you must do it yourself,
it's not about fitness
or even your health.
Good works or hard labor
won't earn it for you,
it's very simple,
it's easy to do—
the things Jesus did
are the main clue,
He did it for me
and He'll do it for you.
While on the cross
He paid our debt,
for the sins we committed
and still will yet.
He died that day
after paying the price,
so, if you're really smart,
you'll take my advice.
It's very simple,
it's easy to do,
I'll tell you now
what you must do—
confess with your mouth
that He did it for you,
believe in your heart
by faith that it's true.
Take up your cross
then follow Him,
this true confession
is where you begin.

It's very simple,
it's easy to do.

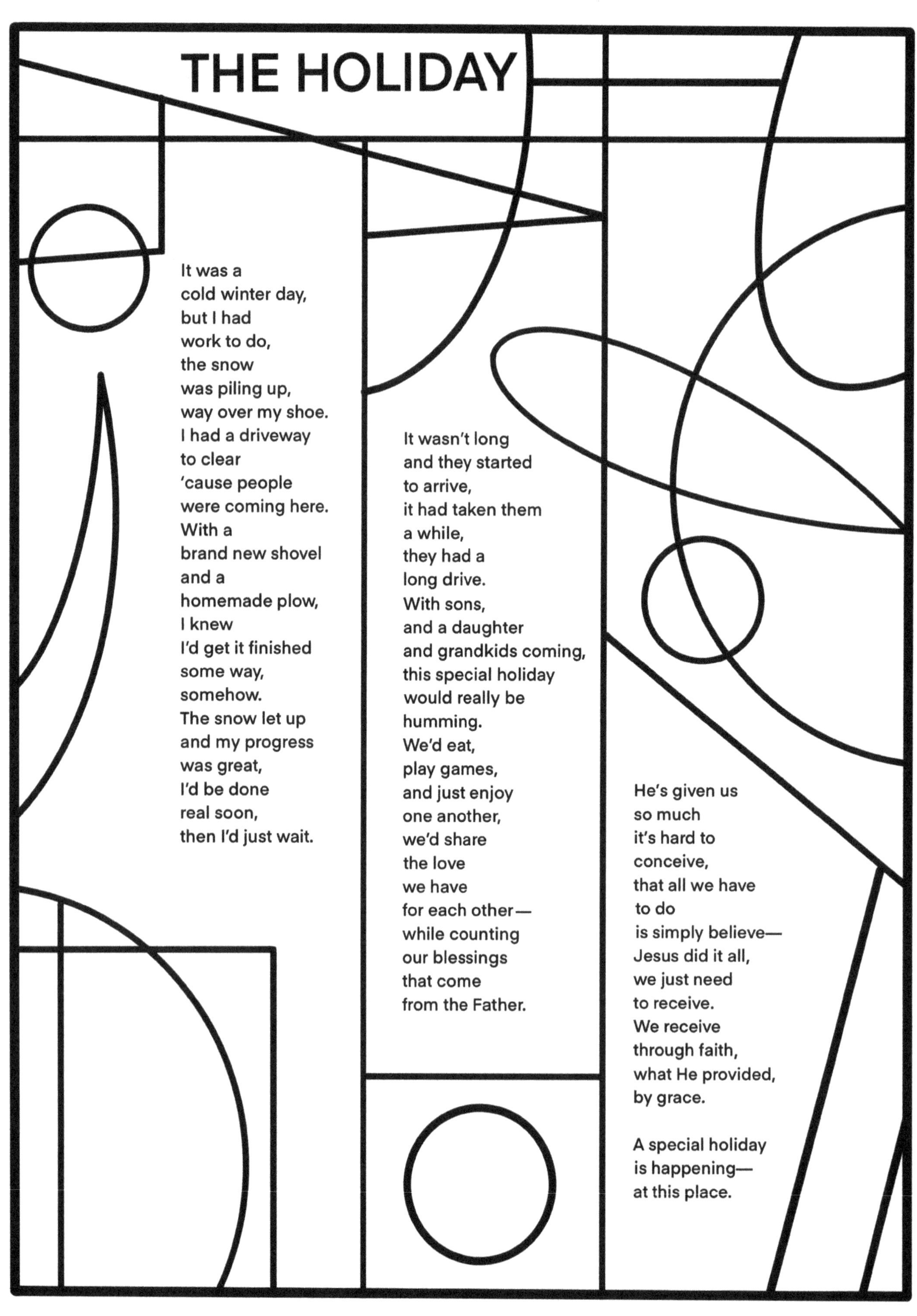

THE HOLIDAY

It was a
cold winter day,
but I had
work to do,
the snow
was piling up,
way over my shoe.
I had a driveway
to clear
'cause people
were coming here.
With a
brand new shovel
and a
homemade plow,
I knew
I'd get it finished
some way,
somehow.
The snow let up
and my progress
was great,
I'd be done
real soon,
then I'd just wait.

It wasn't long
and they started
to arrive,
it had taken them
a while,
they had a
long drive.
With sons,
and a daughter
and grandkids coming,
this special holiday
would really be
humming.
We'd eat,
play games,
and just enjoy
one another,
we'd share
the love
we have
for each other—
while counting
our blessings
that come
from the Father.

He's given us
so much
it's hard to
conceive,
that all we have
to do
is simply believe—
Jesus did it all,
we just need
to receive.
We receive
through faith,
what He provided,
by grace.

A special holiday
is happening—
at this place.

BELIEVE IT OR NOT
Jesus said,
"You must be born
from above."
Believe it or not.
He said,
"I am the way,
the truth, and the life."
Believe it or not.
He said, "If you love me,
you'll obey my commands."
Believe it or not.
He said many other things
that display His love,
He's the very one
who was sent here
from above.
He came down
from the Father
to make men free,
by paying the sin debt—
for you,
and for me.
He lived a perfect life,
then went to the cross,
He offers us salvation,
so we won't be lost.
It's now a free gift for us
if we only believe,
He'll be our savior,
but we have to receive.
Believe it or not.

CHOICES
Life
is filled
with many choices,
if you listen carefully, there are lots of voices.
Some say do this, and others say do that,
do they know what you need,
do they know where you're at?
Some will say go, and some will say stay,
how will you know, what's the right way?
You can search real hard and seek good advice,
some answers come, at a very high price.
When nothing is clear, and you don't know the way,
the obvious choice is simply to pray.
He'll give you direction, you won't be confused,
it's another option, but you have to choose.
Life is filled with many choices,
trust in the Scriptures, and
hear those
voices.

WORDS

Words can be good
or words can be bad.
They can make
you happy
or make you sad.

They can
express devotion
or stir up emotion.
They can be calm
and soothing,
or loud as an ocean.

When spoken softly
they create calm,
or if written poetically,
can express a Psalm.

Musicians use them,
for lyrics to a song;
judges write them,
to right a wrong.

They can be very effective
by the tone of your voice,
however you speak them
is simply your choice.

Words can be important
in times of grief,
when spoken with empathy,
they can bring relief.

Words were used
in the beginning
to create the world,
even outer space,
where all the stars
were hurled.

It all came together
as a master plan,
and it was intended
for the pleasure of man.

Those words were awesome
when said at the first,
now it's up to us
to make them
better or worse.

The Lord doesn't only want us
to do what He wants—
He also wants us
to be what He wants.
In His Word, He says,
"We should obey His commands",
Sometimes He gives us
a right to demand.

He tells us to pray
and that without ceasing,
to continue in His Word
and our faith will keep increasing.
To lay hands on the sick
so they will be healed,
He gave us the Holy Spirit,
by whom we are sealed—
If we invite Him in,
He'll come in for a meal.

When Peter was sinking,
He reached out His hand;
His coming to earth
in the form of a man,
it was all predestined—
it was all in His plan.

Most of that plan
was to take away our sin,
and after that—
for us,
to be like Him.

PREDESTINATION

FEELINGS

Sometimes
you can feel happy or sad.
Sometimes
things can be going good or bad.
Sometimes
your feelings can dominate your life,
depending on events,
or trouble and strife.
Sometimes
things can make you mad,
Sometimes
things can make you glad.
A lot depends on your point of view,
and all of that is controlled by you.
You can see bad things happen
and wonder why;
You can see good things happen
and you might want to cry.
Feelings can be fickle,
it's sad but true.
But then again,
it's all up to you.

Even Jesus—
when Lazarus died...
when He came to his grave,
Jesus cried.
He had tremendous compassion
to heal their ills,
this surely validates
that healing's His will.
Jesus healed—
no matter where He was at,
this brings us comfort,
we can feel good about that.

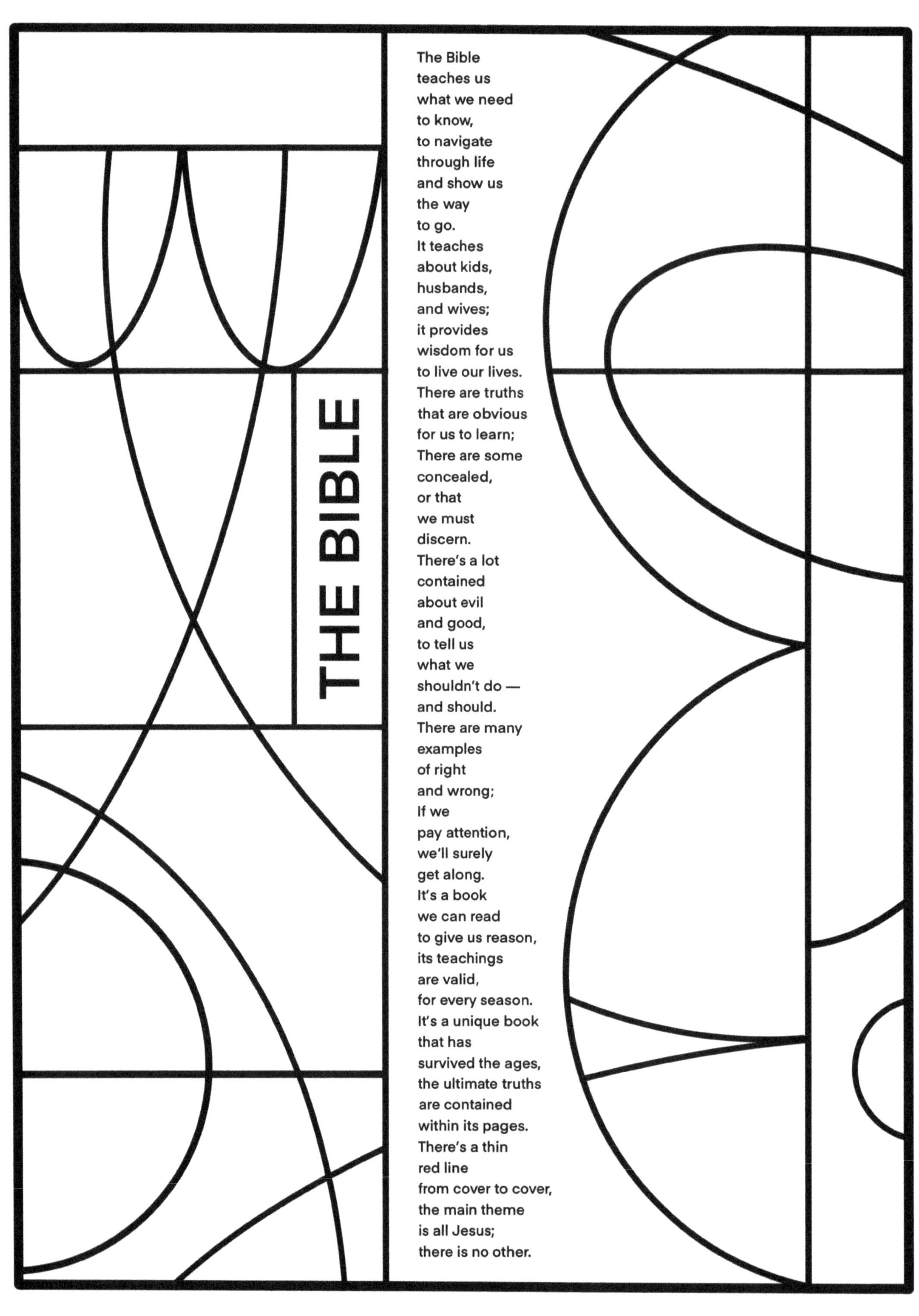
THE BIBLE
The Bible
teaches us
what we need
to know,
to navigate
through life
and show us
the way
to go.
It teaches
about kids,
husbands,
and wives;
it provides
wisdom for us
to live our lives.
There are truths
that are obvious
for us to learn;
There are some
concealed,
or that
we must
discern.
There's a lot
contained
about evil
and good,
to tell us
what we
shouldn't do —
and should.
There are many
examples
of right
and wrong;
If we
pay attention,
we'll surely
get along.
It's a book
we can read
to give us reason,
its teachings
are valid,
for every season.
It's a unique book
that has
survived the ages,
the ultimate truths
are contained
within its pages.
There's a thin
red line
from cover to cover,
the main theme
is all Jesus;
there is no other.

Jesus is God,
He became man.
No one decided that for Him,
it was all in His plan.

He knew man would fall,
even before the start,
But because of His love,
He would do his part;
Even though He knew men
had an evil heart.

He made a creation
where mankind could live,
it was perfectly made,
what else could He give?
He made a universe
so men could sustain,
a perfect environment
without any pain.
He created a man
and it didn't take long,
for man to mess up
and do what was wrong.
The earth became cursed,
Adam gave it away,
he gave up dominion
on that fateful day.
He may not have known
the price Jesus would pay.

Unfortunately, for us,
it's still like that today.

2000 years ago,
redemption was made,
it was a terrible price
Jesus paid.
One of these days
He'll return once again,
to settle the score,
to facilitate Satan's end.
He'll allow the world
to go through great tribulation,
from that time on,
He'll rule the nations.
He'll bring in peace
and a great renovation,
there will be joy on earth
and much celebration!
JESUS IS GOD

PRAISE THE LORD

Sin is described
as missing the mark,
a sinful life
is not a walk
in the park.
Some sins are done
with willful volition,
these are considered
sins of commission,
there are others that are
sins of omission.

Sins of commission
are generally overt acts,
you know they're wrong,
that's a natural fact.

Sins of omission
can be very obscure,
sometimes committed
because you are unsure.

The Holy Spirit will bring
sins to your mind,
repentance is needed
for the peace you'll find.

Confession brings forgiveness
by the grace of the Lord,
(in the Book of 1st John),
you'll find in His Word.

The Lord is gracious
to forgive your sins,
when conviction eases,
you'll know that's when—
your conscience will be clear,
you'll have peace within.
You can confidently
"Praise the Lord" again!

ARE YOU A BELIEVER

Are you a believer
or do you
believe the deceiver?
Have you made up your mind,
or will you be
left behind?
You think it's all good
like a bed of clover—
well, there's coming a day
when it'll soon be over.
Will you be at the Bema Seat of Christ
or the Great White Throne?
Which ever it is,
you'll be there alone.

At the one, is rewards;
The other, condemnation.
There's no chance for a change—
no reconciliations.

What will you say on the fateful day?
If it's the Bema Seat of Christ,
you'll know you're okay.
But if it's the Great White Throne,
there's just no way.

Right now,
you have
a choice
you can make—
so, I'm asking
you now,
what will it take?

Make Jesus your Lord
or go it alone?
But for all of your sins
there is no way to atone.

Heaven or Hell,
it's an obvious choice—
Confess Jesus as Lord,
while you still
have a voice.

REVELATION

What do you think
about the Revelation?
Do you think it's true
or just speculation?
The letters to the churches
aren't just a myth,
they say there's proof
they did really exist.
The Bible says
it's rendered into signs,
some of the things described
can blow your mind.
It's hard for us to fathom
the creatures with wings,
not only those,
but lots of other things.
Beasts with horns
coming out of the sea,
you could ask the question,
"How could that be?"
There are lots of explanations
and some have to be true,
I guess it all depends
on your point of view.

The Bible says it
will last seven years,
it doesn't suggest
any laughter,
but a lot of tears.
It paints an ugly picture
for that entire span,
but in the end,
it culminates
in God's perfect plan.
I, for one,
think it's all true.
If it's not
I haven't lost a thing,
but how about you?
Biblical prophesies
are all the proof I need,
they all come true,
and that satisfies me.

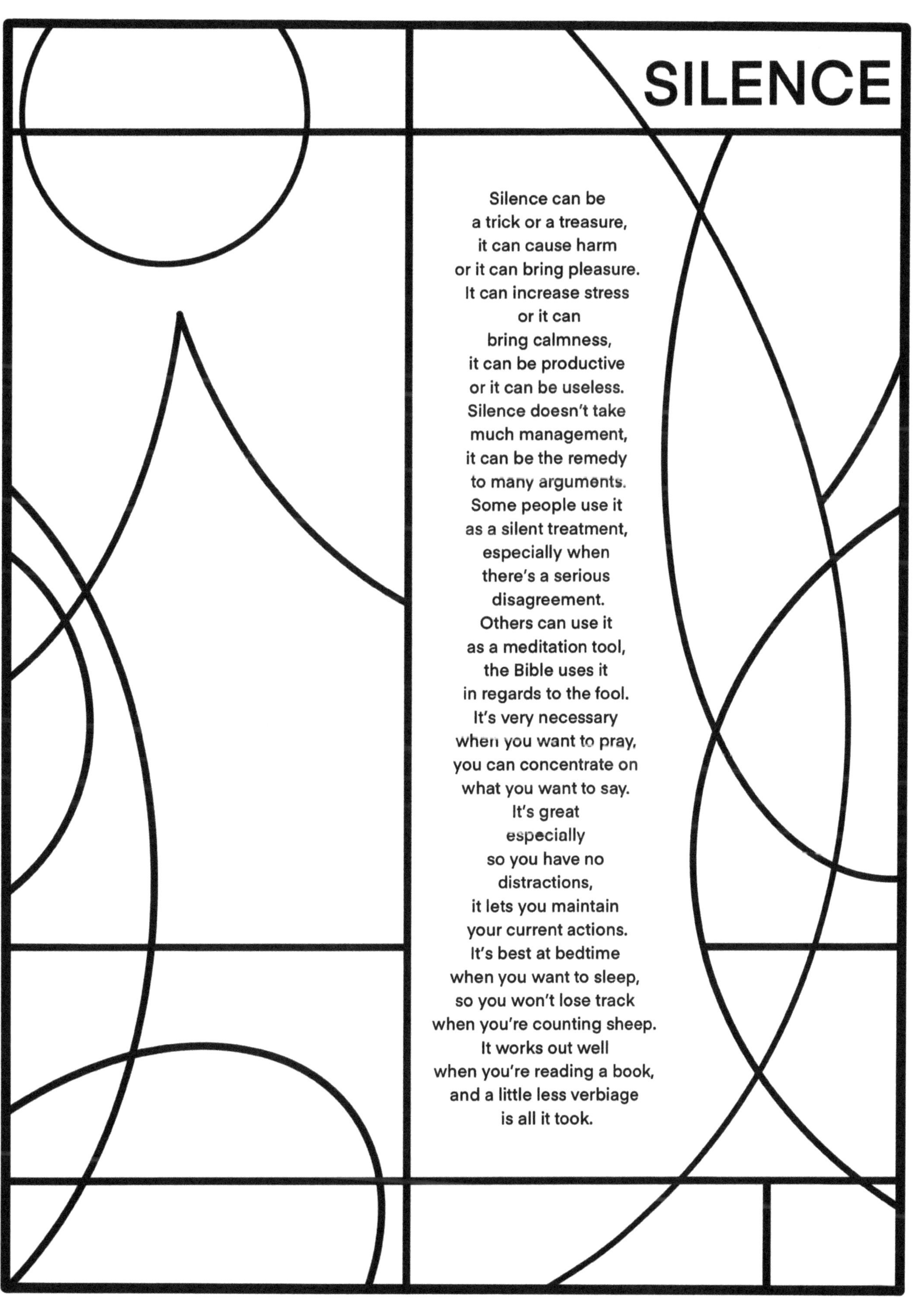

SILENCE

Silence can be
a trick or a treasure,
it can cause harm
or it can bring pleasure.
It can increase stress
or it can
bring calmness,
it can be productive
or it can be useless.
Silence doesn't take
much management,
it can be the remedy
to many arguments.
Some people use it
as a silent treatment,
especially when
there's a serious
disagreement.
Others can use it
as a meditation tool,
the Bible uses it
in regards to the fool.
It's very necessary
when you want to pray,
you can concentrate on
what you want to say.
It's great
especially
so you have no
distractions,
it lets you maintain
your current actions.
It's best at bedtime
when you want to sleep,
so you won't lose track
when you're counting sheep.
It works out well
when you're reading a book,
and a little less verbiage
is all it took.

LIFE

Do you ever wonder
what life is all about?
Do you ever wonder
if it'll all work out?
Will I be rich or poor,
will I even care
anymore?
Will it be entertaining,
or will it be a bore?
Where am I headed,
am I on the right track,
I've gone this far,
it's too late now to turn back.

We're born into this world
with nothing at all,
some of us make it,
and some of us fall.
Some work hard
and strive for success,
whatever that is,
they give it their best.
Some think wealth
will help them pass the test,
without really caring
about any of the rest.

I've noticed a pattern
that is factually true,
everyone dies
when their lifetime is through.

So what's it all mean
when we come to our end?
We'd better know Jesus,
as our best friend.

WAITING

Waiting demands
a lot of patience.
It can test your resolve
in any instance.

My first significant wait
was for going to school,
with siblings ahead of me
I thought it would be cool.
My very first day,
the teacher asked for my lunch money
I carried my lunch,
so I didn't have any.
I started to cry and she said,
"It's all right honey."

The next big wait
wasn't until I reached twelve,
I'd be able to hunt
with my own gun and shells.
As fate would have it
it didn't work out that way,
I had to wait a year,
I don't know why—
even to this day.

Waiting for sixteen
seemed to be out there so far,
I had my permit
and even bought a car.
I finally passed my driver's test,
I was living the dream,
man, this was the best!

Ago twenty-one
was next in my sights,
I'd be an adult
in charge of myself—
for my days and nights.

After all that,
the waits seemed minor to me,
with a family,
then there was responsibility.
Doctor visits, activities, and school,
these became the waits,
as a general rule.

The job was fine, a challenge at times,
but I stayed squared away and toed the line.

Eventually after the kids moved on,
the waiting was over, I needed to proceed on.
Promotions came, with the help of the Lord.
I knew it was Him, because of His Word.

Now I'm retired, but the waiting's not done—
I'm waiting to someday
be with the Son.

Somehow
the universe
was created to be,
it's a natural fact,
as you can clearly see.
There once was nothing,
and then it arrived, with the
planets and stars—they came alive.
Some people say a big bang had occurred,
that may be true, but it's not in God's Word.
He said He made it and called it creation,
even to this day, it brings sure fascination.
His Word is the truth, on that, you can rely,
there's a lot of evidence, they cannot deny.
Somehow it goes on day after day,
it's part of His plan, He designed it that way.
The seasons come and the seasons go,
the spring brings the rain, the winter brings snow.
Somehow it works, year after year,
I thank God I'm alive, and that I'm still here.
But, when it's time for me to make heaven my home,
I'll be happiest there, and I won't be alone.
CREATION

ROADS

Did you ever spend time
thinking about roads?
About cars with people
and trucks with loads.
Traveling to points here
and sometimes there,
or traveling around
just anywhere.
Some roads are dirt
and some are gravel,
some are paved
making it easier to travel.
They can cross over streams
that require bridges,
they can climb hills
and mountains
and cross over ridges.
They can take you almost
anywhere you want to go,
they can get you there fast
or you may have to go slow.
There's real convenience
using freeways and by-ways,
it's especially nice
using interstate highways—
for hauling valuable loads
of trash, or treasure,
or just for a drive
for your family's pleasure.
The roads are fine
while we're living on earth,
but when it comes to eternity,
what are they worth?

Jesus described two,
one narrow, and one wide.
To travel the right one,
you must eliminate pride.
One leads to heaven
and the other to destruction;
If you stay on the second one,
there's no reconstruction.

COLOR

Color, in itself
can be an amazing thing,
it can be pleasing to the eye
or sometimes stings.
Don't look directly
into a welder's torch,
it can injure your eyes
with a burning scorch.
Don't look into the sun
on any day,
it can damage your eyes
in a painful way.
Color is something
special to behold,
it can be faded or bland,
or something bold.
Colors can be signs
to warn us of hazards,
it can be important to know
when it really matters.
A red light flashing
in your rear-view mirror,
it can cause apprehension
or sometimes fear.
The color of blue
can bring lots of joy,
especially when
you've been waiting
for a baby boy.
The yellows and oranges
in the western sky,
display a sunset
that will amaze the eye.
God first displayed the colors
when He created the earth—
to show its value,
to express its worth.
The softest shades
express His love,
the bolder colors,
indicate justice above.

I'm glad He didn't
make it just
black and white,
I think He felt
it just wouldn't be right.

FIRE

The Bible often mentions fire—
it can be a warming influence,
if that's your desire.
It can warm your house,
and dry your clothes,
cook your meals,
and even warm your toes.
There are many uses
you can avail,
you can burn your campfire
in an old rusty pail.

Fire can wreak havoc
when not kept in check,
if it happens when grilling outside,
it could burn your deck.
A forest can burn
and leave everything charred,
it can damage the trees
and leave them permanently scarred.

Peter warmed by a fire
while denying the Lord,
a girl called him out,
but he denied with his words.

Elijah called down fire
from heaven above,
then killed all of the prophets
that Jezebel loved.

These kinds of fires
didn't cause any harm,
but I'm here today
to sound the alarm.

Jesus warns of a fire
that burns as a lake,
if you ever end up there
there's no escape.
It'll burn forever
and never quit—
Accept Jesus now,
so you don't
end up in it.

THE THIEF ON THE CROSS

What about
the thief on the cross?
Up to that point,
he knew he was lost.
He talked to Jesus
and made his plea,
if not on the cross
he'd have gone on a knee.
He knew he was sentenced
and destined to die,
there were no questions,
he surely knew why.
He was fortunate that day
because of God's grace,
now the Great White
Throne judgement,
he'd not have to face.
Jesus showed mercy
by setting him free—
He said, "Today you'll be
in paradise with me."
The other thief,
we know not his name,
but obviously his fate
just wasn't the same.
The chance for paradise
had just slipped by,
there's no need to ask,
we all know why.

So humble yourself
and swallow your pride,
take this opportunity,
don't run and hide.
He'll welcome you in
and take you aboard,
then you'll have
the privilege of
calling Him Lord.

THE RICH MAN

The rich man knew
he had it made,
he threw out scraps
where the beggar laid.
The dogs came around
and licked his sores,
we can know for sure—
he was very poor.
Lazarus was
the poor man's name,
the way things were
he had no claim to fame.
He eventually died
and was carried away,
to Abraham's bosom
where he'd be able to stay.
Finally, also,
the rich man died,
he was buried —
but went
to the other side.
At this place,
there was a gap
no one could cross;
The saved, with Abraham —
the others were lost.
He cried out to Abraham
to get some relief,
we know he was there
because of his unbelief.
He had five brothers
he wanted to save,
he asked him to
send someone
back from the grave,
to tell them how
to avoid this place—
a noble request,
even showing some grace.
But they had Moses
and the prophets
who they could hear,
if they listened to them,
they won't end up here.

Now we have Jesus—
who came back from the grave,
if you accept Him today,
you'll surely be saved.

SOWING & REAPING

In your lifetime now,
what are you sowing?
Do you know for sure
where you are going?
Is it good seed or bad,
do you know if it's growing?

Are you getting anything done
or just spinning your wheels?
Are you satisfied with your progress,
how do you feel?
The Word of God
is the seed
you must sow,
sometimes the soil
will not let it grow.
Jesus never said quit—
so we still gotta go.

With the signs of the times
I think the end is near,
with all the noise in the world,
it's hard for people to hear.
There are hearts out there
you don't want to be around,
but we also know
there's a lot of fertile ground.

So do what you can,
give it your best shot—
tell them the truth,
they can believe it or not.
The way you live
your daily life,
is a reflection of Jesus,
especially when there's strife.

Paul was a witness
who gave it his all,
he wouldn't quit,
they couldn't make him fall.
We must be like him—
and answer the call.

When it comes to the Gospel,
we've got to stand tall.

HOT OR COLD

Let me ask you,
are you weak or bold?

When it comes to the Gospel,
are you hot or cold?

What would people say about you
if the truth be told?
Do you take it with you,
wherever you go—
if you met up with strangers,
would they even know?

When it comes to the Gospel,
are you hot or cold?

Do you ever witness
or tell people your story?
Do you explain it clearly,
so God gets the glory?
A lot of people
go to church on Sunday,
you'd never know they were
Christians, on Monday.

When it comes to the Gospel,
are you hot or cold?

Jesus said, He'd rather you
be one or the other—
I think if you're not,
you'd better run for cover.
There'll be no place to go
and no place to hide,
give your life to Him,
and forget about pride.

When it comes to the Gospel,
are you hot or cold?

Telling your story,
what God's done for you,
is not hard at all
if it's factually true.
You can never measure
how much you gave,
you might have just gotten
somebody saved.

When it comes to the Gospel,
are you hot or cold?

So you're a rich man,
and you want to go to heaven?
It's not impossible, but you must
be aware of the Pharisees' leaven.
It doesn't depend on your money or wealth,
it's not about your social status, or even your health.
Money can be a good servant, a useful tool,
you can buy expensive clothes and look real cool.
You can buy Rolex watches and diamond rings,
Cadillacs, and all kinds of other expensive things.
You can buy expensive food, travel to faraway places,
but when you see all these people,
will you remember their faces?
The luxuries on earth could all be yours,
and here in this life, money can open lots of doors.
All of this, by itself, will not please the Master,
do things for the kingdom, and do them much faster.
It's all about the heart and His great love,
do all that you do, for Jesus, the Lord up above.
Salvation is not earned by money or works,
it's a gift of God, it's one of the perks.
So don't love your money, love Jesus instead,
put Him number one in your life,
and you'll be way ahead.
CAN A RICH MAN GO TO HEAVEN?

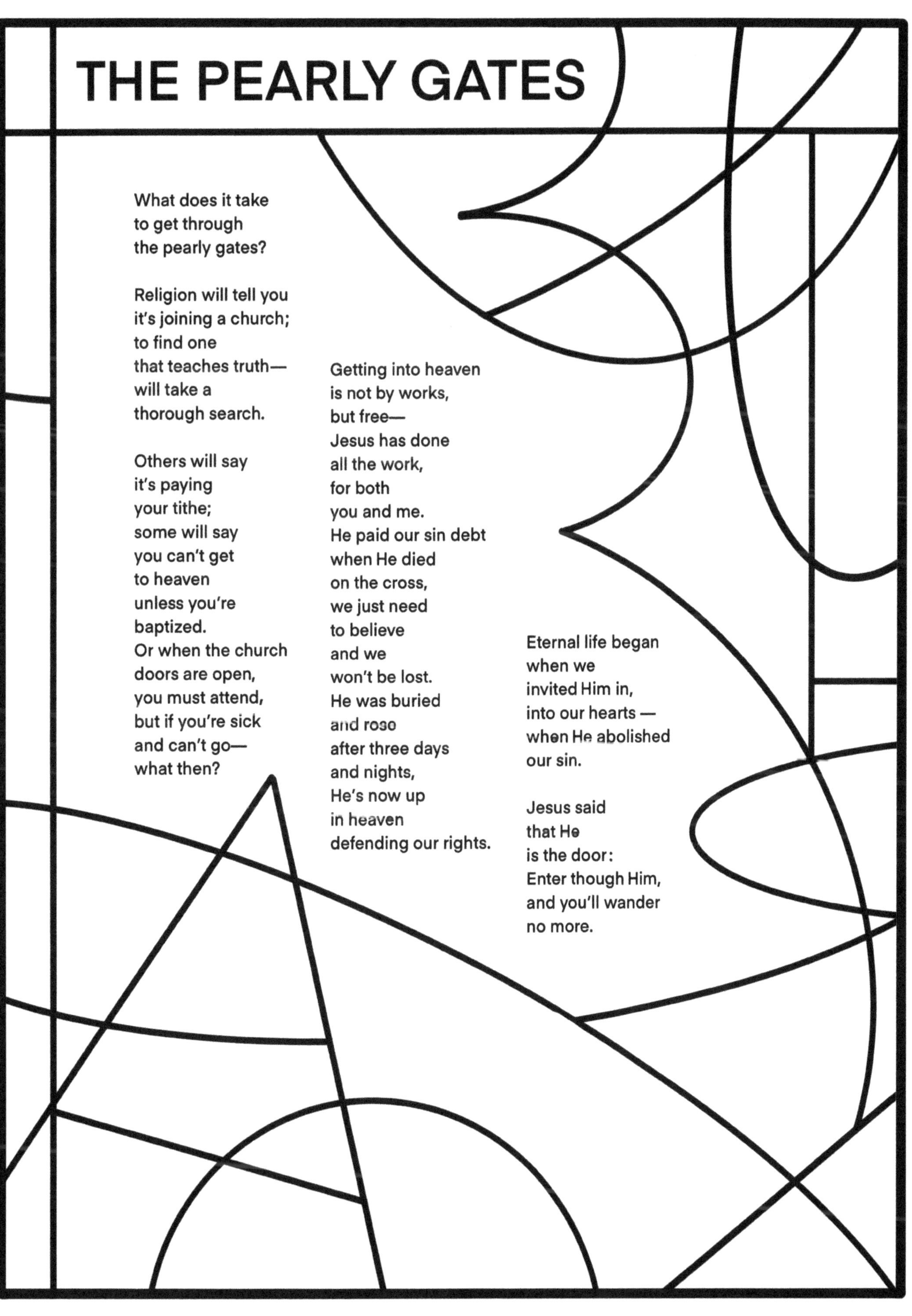

THE PEARLY GATES

What does it take
to get through
the pearly gates?

Religion will tell you
it's joining a church;
to find one
that teaches truth—
will take a
thorough search.

Others will say
it's paying
your tithe;
some will say
you can't get
to heaven
unless you're
baptized.
Or when the church
doors are open,
you must attend,
but if you're sick
and can't go—
what then?

Getting into heaven
is not by works,
but free—
Jesus has done
all the work,
for both
you and me.
He paid our sin debt
when He died
on the cross,
we just need
to believe
and we
won't be lost.
He was buried
and rose
after three days
and nights,
He's now up
in heaven
defending our rights.

Eternal life began
when we
invited Him in,
into our hearts —
when He abolished
our sin.

Jesus said
that He
is the door:
Enter though Him,
and you'll wander
no more.

THE HEART

What do you believe
about your heart?
When mentioned in Scripture,
it's a critical part.
It's obviously a blood pump,
that's plain to see,
when it was created,
that's what it was meant to be.
But there's a deeper issue,
like the heart of a tree—
it's really our spirit
inside of you and me.
It's the core of our being,
it's who we are—
we can be lowly,
exceptional,
or even just par;
if you're reading this,
you've made it this far.

The heart has been evil
inside of man,
it was created in love,
that's how it began.
Jesus told Nicodemus,
"You must be born from above."
He was trying to get us back
to a position of love—
to change our condition
and how we survive,
a born-again experience,
to make us alive.

"To walk by faith
and not by sight",
to rest in His reassurance,
by day and by night.

FATHERHOOD

If you've never been a father,
you may not understand,
how sometimes
it's really tough
to be the man.
Some events happen
not under your control,
it can happen to policemen
when they're out on patrol.
You investigate an accident
and you know people will die,
sometime if it's children
you might want to cry.
But you suck it all up,
it's what you're expected to do,
you say a quick prayer,
and the Lord pulls you through;
you thank Him again,
for taking care of you.

A fireman knows
this same kind of pain,
a structure fire—
with children within.
He tries his hardest
to be strong and brave,
there are children inside—
he's expected to save.
Sometimes he can't,
that's a terrible shame,
he gave it his best,
he's not to blame.

A little girl
gets hit by a car
and survives,
you pray real hard
and thank God,
she's alive.
She recovers in time
and becomes a success,
that's when you know
it's God
at His best.

JESUS WORK

When Jesus died upon the cross,
that was one giant step in Satan's loss.
He paid the debt for all our sin,
He'll never have to do it again.
When He went to the grave, Satan thought he had won,
but on the fourth day when he looked in,
Jesus was gone;
Satan was foiled again.

Jesus won
and Satan lost.
Glory to God
and the heavenly host.

He's in heaven now, at the Father's right hand,
waiting patiently, for the Father's command—
to come back for His church and take them home,
you better be on his side or you'll be left alone.

He'll let the earth suffer great tribulation,
then He'll end it—
and bring rehabilitation.

Praise God for His great plan!

Praise God for redeeming man!

When it comes
to the Rapture,
what will they say—
that aliens came
and took them away?
Why only Christians—
did they all pray?
They said it was in the Bible,
it would happen someday.
There's a lot of preachers left,
why didn't they go?
It's a real mystery,
we may never know.
The Rapture is said
to be a great snatching away—
it's written in the Bible,
in a subtle way.
The Lord will come back
and remain in the sky,
He'll call the Christians to come
without a goodbye.
In the blink of an eye,
they'll be changed—
and won't die;
though they don't have wings,
they're destined to fly.
They've been taken to safety
to walk on golden paths—
the reason, He said,
was to avoid His great wrath.
The destruction predicted
to come on the earth—
the worst one ever,
since the time it was cursed.
If you don't believe,
I suggest you study,
because when it happens—
there's no time to get ready.
THE RAPTURE

CONCLUSION

I want you to know
there is a point to all this:
for you to accept
Jesus as Savior,
is my personal wish.

Me and my family
did this years ago,
we all love Jesus
and want
people to know.

It's made a
tremendous difference
in all of our lives,
It's been good for us men,
and all of our wives.
It's not just us,
but our daughters besides.

We've all had struggles
at times in our lives,
but whenever it's happened,
we've always survived.

Everything hasn't been perfect,
by any means,
and when we look back
Jesus was always on the scene.
He's always been there
through thick and thin,
we know for sure
He'll be there,
again and again.

So as I pray for you
down on my knees,
I know I can't force you,
so I'll ask you please—
consider my request;
and give it your best.

ABOUT THE AUTHOR

James B. Kockler grew up in
Western Pennsylvania and
spent his early working years
in construction, and as a draftsman,
before joining the
Pennsylvania State Police in 1968—
where he served with distinction.
After retiring as a Lieutenant in 1994,
he now lives a quiet life in rural Pennsylvania
with his wife. He enjoys fishing, hunting,
attending Bible study, and spending time
with his family, including nine grandchildren
and eight great-grandchildren.

www.ingramcontent.com/pod-product-compliance
Lightning Source LLC
LaVergne TN
LVHW060642110826
845147LV00018B/1025

* 9 7 9 8 3 8 5 2 7 9 6 4 7 *